Sacred STILLNESS

A Women's Lenten
Devotional Journal

Abingdon *Women*

A WOMEN'S LENTEN DEVOTIONAL JOURNAL

Copyright © 2025 Abingdon Press
All rights reserved.

978-1-7910-4070-3

Cover Decscription: The cover of *Sacred Stillness: A Women's Lenten Devotional Journal* features a tranquil watercolor-style landscape. A soft mist rises over a calm pond bordered by smooth stones and leafy plants. A small wooden bridge crosses the water on the left, and delicate branches of a blossoming tree extend from the upper right corner, dotted with pale pink flowers and green buds. Birds glide peacefully in the distance and one perches on a branch, adding to the sense of serenity. The title appears in elegant serif type: the words *sacred* in soft green and *stillness* in black capital letters. Below, in a muted rose-color the text, reads "A Women's Lenten Devotional Journal."

MANUFACTURED IN THE UNITED STATES OF AMERICA

CONTENTS

INTRODUCTION

In our world of constant motion and endless noise, the ancient call to be still before God feels both more challenging and more necessary than ever before. Yet in our hurried age, we often approach our spiritual disciplines with the same restless energy that characterizes our daily lives. This devotional invites you into a transformative forty-day journey through the Lenten season (or Lent)—a time when believers turn inward to examine their hearts, confess their shortcomings, and lean into the profound mystery of Easter, where silence becomes the backdrop in which you can walk on the path toward deeper communion with the Trinity.

Each day's reflection in *Sacred Stillness* utilizes many of the Scriptures used in the Revised Common Lectionary, a three-year cycle of readings many churches use to organize their worship and ensure that they're reading the same Bible passages each Sunday as other churches around the world. Drawing from this rich tradition, these meditations will guide you beyond mere religious activity into authentic encounter with God's presence. You will discover that stillness is not emptiness. It is not the absence of God but the spaciousness to receive divine love more completely.

The forty devotions that follow include a brief Scripture passage, a meditational thought, a prayer you can offer, and discussion questions for further reflection as you go into your day. Whether you are a seasoned contemplative or someone new to a slower way of reading and responding to Scripture, these pages offer gentle guidance into the transformative power of sacred stillness.

As you begin this Lenten pilgrimage, remember that the goal is not spiritual achievement but spiritual awakening, not doing more but being more present to the One who is always present to you.

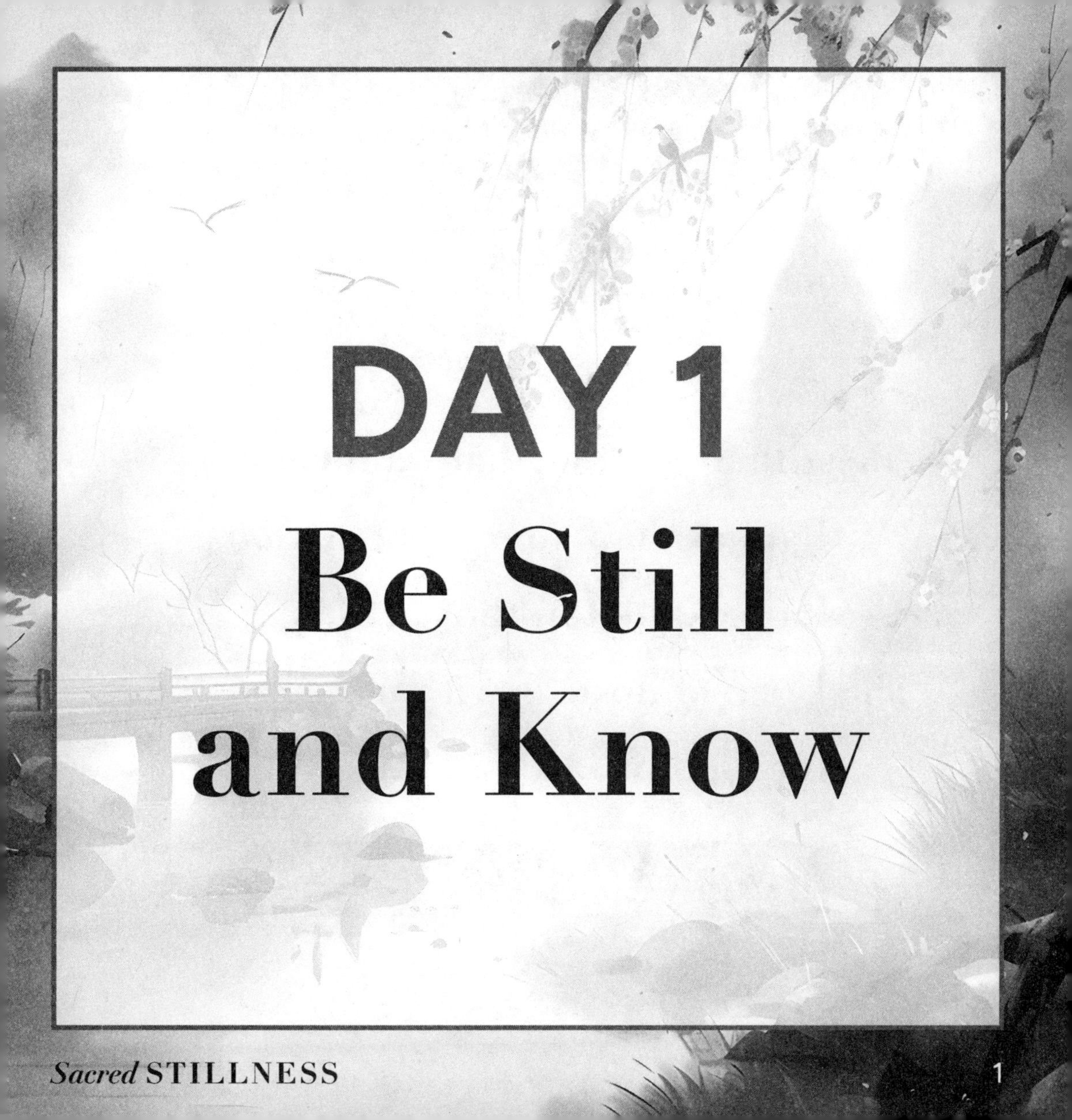

DAY 1

Be Still and Know

"Be still, and know that I am God!

I am exalted among the nations;

I am exalted in the earth."

The LORD of hosts is with us;

the God of Jacob is our refuge.

Psalm 46:10-11 NRSVue

From the first chapters of Genesis, we see God seek out a personal relationship with His children built on trust and obedience. God called out characters like Moses, Gideon, Elijah, and Abraham and Sarah to follow Him in faith, not knowing what the outcome would be. Their lives demonstrated both their faithfulness and their fear. They trusted God until they didn't. Their faith was a work in progress.

In this psalm, God encourages His people (then and now) to cease striving and trust that He is big enough to care for their needs, large and small. God is refuge and strength to those who cling to Him (v. 1). Later we hear Jesus offer the same plea: "Trust in God. Trust also in me" (John 14:1). Jesus, the incarnation of God in the world, calls for His followers to trust Him. Jesus can see what is ahead and He has our hands, so He can guide us safely. The truth is we are a lot like the biblical characters we read in the pages of Scripture. We trust God until we don't. Our faith is a work in progress too.

The season of Lent offers time for us to be still and remember just how awesome God is—and how much He wants to lead and provide for us. When we stop striving and grasping to secure an outcome that seems best for us, we can surrender ourselves to our heavenly Father who knows what we need before we ask.

PRAYER

Lord, help me stop and be still before You and remember that You are God Almighty. You know all things and can do all things according to Your perfect plan. When fear creeps up and I am tempted to doubt You, remind me of Your faithfulness in generations past. I ask for the faith to surrender. In this season, quiet my soul to know that You are Sovereign, and You hold my life secure in Your loving hands. Amen.

In what areas of your life do you struggle to trust God?

Sacred STILLNESS

What would it be like for you to be still before God?

What can you do to incorporate silence and stillness into your daily life?

DAY 2

Waiting Can Be Good

The LORD is good to those who hope in him, to the person who seeks him. It's good to wait in silence for the LORD's deliverance.

Lamentations 3:25-26

The Book of Lamentations provides us a model for how to pray when everything in our world has fallen to pieces and we do not know how to move forward. Written after Babylon destroyed Jerusalem and the people were left to rebuild their homes and lives, it models honest and authentic prayer. The pleas and questions reflect deep anguish and confusion. We can follow their example in our own prayers to name our deepest pains and to utter our darkest fears, trusting that God will listen and respond.

Sometimes we lose sight of God's goodness and faithfulness. We yearn for a response from God, but God seems silent and so far away. In those times, we can follow in the footsteps of those who have gone before us, crying out to God from our pain and waiting in faith for God to act. In doing so, our prayers of lament can draw us closer to God and God's healing grace. We can rest assured that God sees and hears even when He seems silent. When we cling to this truth, we, too, can lift our heads—even if just for a moment— and say, "There is hope."

Sacred STILLNESS

PRAYER

God, thank You for hearing my deepest cries. You don't chastise me for my honesty or rebuke me for my questions. You allow me to voice my anger and my fears. When my world is chaotic and nothing makes sense, give me the grace to wait for Your deliverance. Help me remember your heart toward me and trust that even if I cannot see the road ahead, You are already there. Amen.

Use this space to tell God about something chaotic or confusing in your life.

When has God brought you out of a dark and difficult time? Describe how God cared for you.

Can you think of someone who needs to hear words of hope in their current situation? What encouragement might you offer them?

DAY 3
God
Waits
Too

Nonetheless, the LORD is waiting to be

merciful to you,

and will rise up to show you

compassion.

The LORD is a God of justice;

happy are all who wait for him.

Isaiah 30:18

Sacred STILLNESS

Mercy is a primary characteristic of God in the Old Testament. God led the people of Israel out of slavery in Egypt because of His mercy. He made a covenant promise to treat them with faithfulness, compassion, patience, and kindness (Exodus 34:1-10). And in the New Testament, the apostle Paul noted that we can do nothing to earn God's mercy; God shows mercy to people because He chooses to do so. Doing the "right" things like going to church, serving people, and avoiding sin cannot earn God's mercy. These things are good, and Christians should do them. But they flow from our freedom obtained by Christ (Romans 8:1-17), not to gain God's forgiveness or favor.

God is radically inclusive in granting mercy, often using unexpected people to fulfill God's purposes, including the rebellious Israelites described in Isaiah 30. And God continues to include seemingly unlikely people as recipients and heralds of God's grace and forgiveness—people like you and me. Despite our propensity to turn away from God, He wants to show mercy and waits for us to turn to Him. God wants to use us to extend His mercy to others too. During this season, let God's faithfulness, compassion, patience, and kindness flow through you because He continually offers them to you.

PRAYER

Thank You, Lord, for continually extending Your mercy toward me. I can never exhaust the storehouses of Your love, grace, and compassion. You never stop caring about me, even when I can't feel your nearness. Give me the opportunity to extend your mercy toward others and mirror Your love for people. Show me times when I take your faithfulness for granted and develop in me a deeper awareness of your mercy toward me. Amen.

How has God extended mercy toward you lately?

How might today's reading change your perspective about God's mercy?

How has your understanding of God's mercy changed over time?

DAY 4
Search
and
Rescue

Then Jesus said to him, "Today salvation has come to this house, because he, too, is a son of Abraham. For the Son of Man came to seek out and to save the lost."

Luke 19:9-10 (NRSVue)

You are probably familiar with the story of Zacchaeus in the Bible. He was a chief tax collector, so he was rich but not popular. This is because he gained his wealth at the expense of others. The crowds called him a "sinner" (19:7). Zacchaeus went to great lengths to meet Jesus, perhaps because he knew that despite his wealth, his life was even smaller than his stature. He was determined to lay eyes on the man who was called "a friend of tax collectors and sinners" (Luke 7:34). Who is this Jesus who aligns Himself with people living in the margins?

By reaching out, speaking Zacchaeus's name, and going to visit him, Jesus offered Zacchaeus a relationship. Zacchaeus discovered that he could go from being an oppressor and despised man to a beloved child of God, worth more than all the riches he could embezzle.

We can experience the same transformative power as we turn from our sin and pursue a relationship with Jesus. And as we continually bear our hearts before the One who knows us completely, He transforms us into the people He created us to be.

PRAYER

Heavenly Father, thank You for pursuing a relationship with me. Your love continues to transform me. I am grateful that I am not bound to my past mistakes, but that You cleanse me and give me a new path to walk. Give me the confidence in knowing You love me and are making me more like the person You created me to be.

When you reflect on your life, how has Jesus pursued a relationship with you?

Describe a time when you felt an overwhelming sense of God's forgiveness.

How can you extend the same forgiveness and grace to someone in your life?

DAY 5
Reaching Out for Jesus

It's not that I have already reached this goal or have already been perfected, but I pursue it, so that I may grab hold of it because Christ grabbed hold of me for just this purpose. Brothers and sisters, I myself don't think I've reached it, but I do this one thing: I forget about the things behind me and reach out for the things ahead of me. The goal I pursue is the prize of God's upward call in Christ Jesus.

Philippians 3:12-14

People make assumptions about our worth based on our bodies—our appearance, our shape, our fitness, and what we can accomplish as embodied women—but that is not God's way.

In Philippians 3:7-9, Paul listed all physical and social assets that marked him as a person of high regard and status, but he willingly rejected them all because his relationship with Christ was worth even more. He did not think he had it all together or had arrived at some higher spiritual plane. He knew his pursuit of Christ was lifelong, and he was determined to live as a faithful follower of Jesus.

What was true for Paul is true for us today. Pursuing a life consistent with God's "upward call" (3:14), rather than by the world's standards, is possible by the power of Christ living in us through the Holy Spirit. Like Paul, we can forget about what is behind—past sin, addictions, mistakes, prejudices, and strongholds—and chase after Jesus as He calls us into a deeper and stronger relationship with Him.

PRAYER

Jesus, the world measures my worth by my appearance, accomplishments, and productivity, but You call me to something infinitely better. Like Paul, I choose to count the things of this world as rubbish compared to knowing You. Help me forget my past failures and mistakes and accept the life You invite me to experience. Fill me with Your Spirit so I can chase after You with my whole heart. Amen.

What things distract You from pursuing Jesus?

Sacred STILLNESS

How is pursuing a life with Jesus countercultural in our world today?

How might your life be different if you were able to forget about the things behind you and reach out for what is ahead of you—a life with Jesus?

DAY 6
Creating a Clean Heart

Hide your face from my sins;
   wipe away all my guilty deeds!
Create a clean heart for me, God;
   put a new, faithful spirit deep
   inside me!

Psalm 51:9-10

Psalm 51 is a soulful lament by someone who needs forgiveness and mercy. The first nine verses are full of language about the sin that the psalmist has committed: "my wrongdoings," "my guilt," and "my sin."

God longs for "truth in the most hidden places" (51:6), but the power of sin is not the final word. Even as the psalmist admitted their guilt, they appealed to God's grace. The first words of the psalm introduce this dynamic: "Have mercy on me, God."

Even as the psalmist acknowledged that all humans do wrong, he stated that only God can put it right. God is the one to whom we cry out, "Wipe away all my guilty deeds! Create a clean heart for me" (51:9-10). In this new reality—with God's gift of a new heart and a new spirit—the broken one is transformed into a witness of God's transforming grace.

As we walk through the season of Lent, we can acknowledge our sinfulness just as this psalmist did, but we can also thank God for unlimited mercy and faithful love that draws us back to Him. And like the psalmist, we can live in such a way as to draw others to the foot of the cross and receive forgiveness, mercy, and grace too.

PRAYER

Lord, I know I have failed and fallen short of your commands. I've made decisions that have hurt You and others. I desperately need Your mercy and forgiveness. Wash me clean from the inside out. Transform my heart into one that truly seeks You. Fill me with Your Spirit and help me walk forward in wholeness with renewed purpose. Let my life point others to You. Amen.

What do you need to confess to God today?

This psalm is a lament of someone faced with the depth of the harm their actions have inflicted. How have your actions or words affected those around you?

How do you feel knowing God chooses to cleanse you from your sin through Christ's sacrifice?

DAY 7
Saving
Your Life

After calling the crowd together with his disciples, Jesus said to them, "All who want to come after me must say no to themselves, take up their cross, and follow me. All who want to save their lives will lose them. But all who lose their lives because of me and because of the good news will save them. Why would people gain the whole world but lose their lives?"

Mark 8:34-36

In this passage, Jesus described faithfulness as a dying to self and taking up our cross so we can make Jesus the center of our lives as we follow Him. Doing this requires self-sacrifice, but how women live that out may look different based on their background, life situation, and cultural context. For those of us with an abundance of resources and power, faithfulness may look like humbling ourselves and setting aside our own desires so we can serve others. In this way, we can become like Christ as He washed the feet of his disciples.

For women who are regularly expected or forced to give up our desires to those in power, faithfulness takes on a different pattern. Many women are not treated with the dignity that comes with being made in God's image. For them faithfulness looks more like setting aside self-hatred and fear. It means embracing the knowledge that they are God's beloved.

No matter our circumstances, Jesus calls us to give our lives—our past, present, and future—to Him and seek His desires for our lives.

PRAYER

Jesus, You call me to take up my cross and follow You. Whether I need to humble my pride and serve others, or reject self-hatred and embrace my worth as Your beloved, show me what faithfulness looks like in my life. Help me die to selfish desires and live for Yours. I give You my past failures, present struggles, and future dreams. Be the center of my life as I seek to become like You. Amen.

What does faithfulness to Jesus look like in your life?

What are you holding on to in your life that is keeping you from gaining life in Christ?

What would it look like for you to "say no" to yourself?

DAY 8
The Joy of Forgiveness

The one whose wrongdoing is forgiven,

  whose sin is covered over, is truly happy!

The one the LORD doesn't consider guilty—

  in whose spirit there is no dishonesty—

  that one is truly happy!

Psalm 32:1-2

Joy is not a word the world often associates with religion. Many think religion is solemn, boring, and legalistic, and it frowns upon the things that bring us joy. There's a reason they call what happens at the bar between 4–6 p.m. "happy hour" and what happens on Sunday morning the "Sunday service." The world pictures a system of do's and don'ts or a sin management program rather than a life of abundance.

Joy is not about what we can do, but what God can do and has done for us in Christ. The psalmist understood that the source of joy comes from being forgiven and loved by God Almighty, our Creator. If our joy is focused on things we can do on our own or what we can provide for ourselves, then our joy will last only as long as our money or ability holds out. However, when being forgiven by Jesus is the center of our joy, we can still savor that joy when our circumstances change or our faith falters. We can have joy regardless of our situations in life because we can know and rely on the love God has for us (1 John 4:16).

PRAYER

Merciful God, I am grateful for Your unfailing forgiveness. You brought me out of the depths of my sin into freedom and peace. Teach me to walk in honesty, to trust You fully, and to follow Your guidance. Keep me from chasing after false gods that lure me away, and surround me with Your steadfast love. Let my life reflect the joy of being redeemed and restored by Your grace. Amen.

What temptations or sinful habits lure you away from Jesus?

How do you feel when the weight of sin wears you down?

How do you feel when you confess your sin?

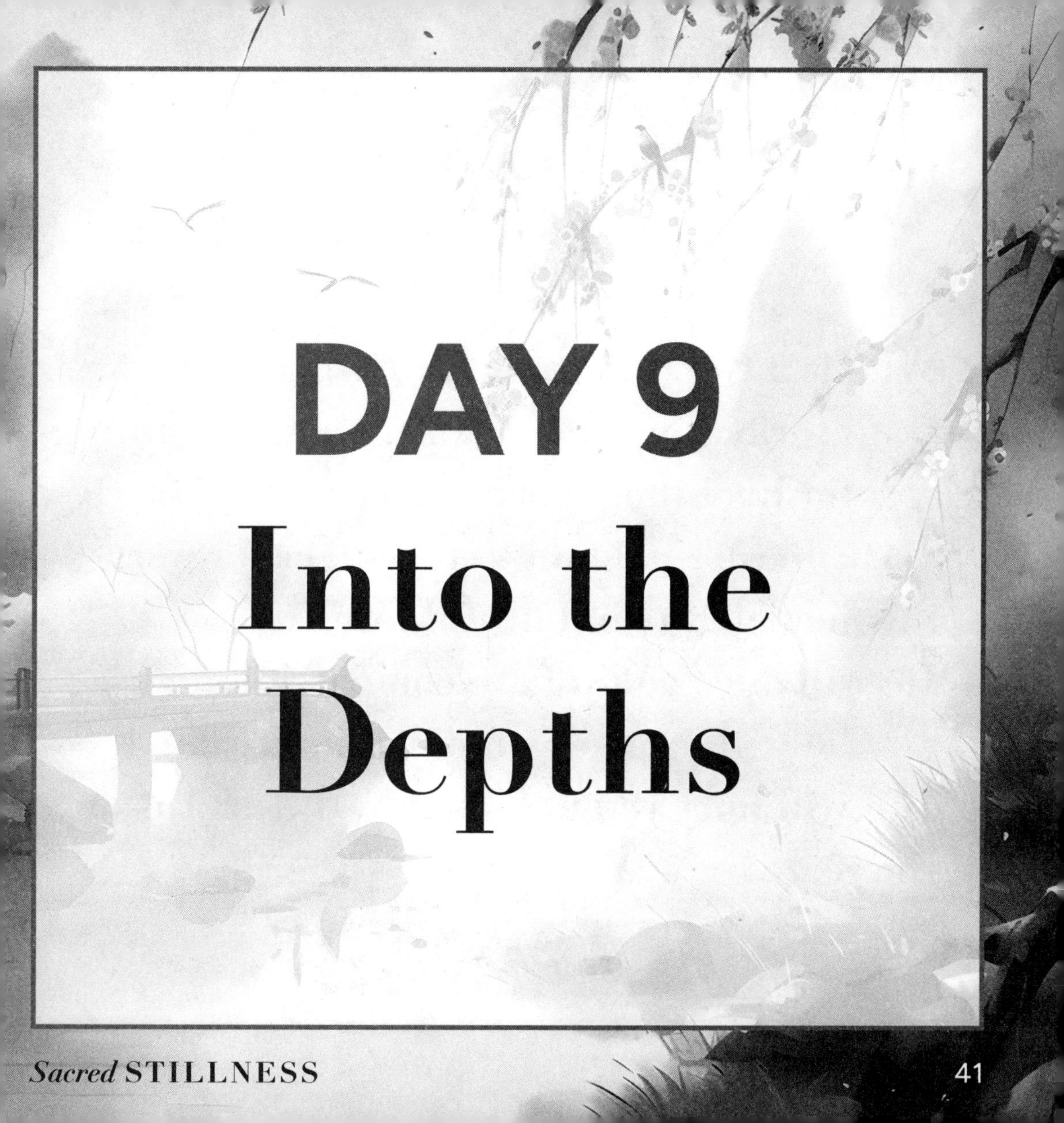

DAY 9

Into the Depths

Who is a God like you, pardoning iniquity,
    overlooking the sin of the few remaining
    for his inheritance?
  He doesn't hold on to his anger forever;
    he delights in faithful love.
He will once again have compassion on us;
    he will tread down our iniquities.
You will hurl all our sins into the depths of
the sea.

Micah 7:18-19

In these closing verses of Micah, the prophet marvels at God's character with a question that echoes through eternity: "Who is a God like you?" And here we discover the stunning answer.

Our God is wholly other not only because of His power and majesty but also because of His mercy. While human anger burns long and seeks revenge, God does not stay angry forever. Instead, He delights in mercy—it brings Him joy to forgive!

During Lent, we walk through forty days of reflection, repentance, and preparation for Easter. This season calls us to examine our hearts, confess our sin, and remember our desperate need for grace. Micah reminds us that our God doesn't merely tolerate our return—He celebrates it. God treads our sins underfoot like a warrior crushing enemies, then hurls them into the depths of the sea where they vanish forever. Our shame, guilt, and rebellion are resurrected as faith, hope, and love.

Let this truth anchor our souls: we serve a God who delights in mercy, whose compassion triumphs over judgment, and whose love casts our sins away.

PRAYER

God of unmatched mercy, who is like You? In Your great love, You choose compassion over wrath and welcome me back when I stray. As I reflect and repent during Lent, remind me that You do not hold anger forever—you delight to forgive. Crush my sin beneath Your feet and let me walk confidently and humbly in Your grace. Let Your love transform my shame into a story of hope that I can share with others. Amen.

How would you answer the question "Who is like God?"

How do you feel knowing that God hurls your sins away from you like an object thrown into the depths of the ocean?

How can your shame or regret become a story of hope for someone who needs to know about God's deep mercy?

DAY 10
Holy and Blameless

Bless the God and Father of our Lord Jesus Christ! He has blessed us in Christ with every spiritual blessing that comes from heaven. God chose us in Christ to be holy and blameless in God's presence before the creation of the world. God destined us to be his adopted children through Jesus Christ because of his love. This was according to his goodwill and plan.

Ephesians 1:3-5

During Lent, we often focus on what we will give up for forty days. Yet Paul's opening words in Ephesians remind us that our relationship with God begins not with our efforts, but with His choice. Before the world existed, before sin entered creation, before we drew our first breath, God had already set His sights on us as the object of His love.

God's decision to make us holy and blameless is not based on our merit or potential—it flows from God's "goodwill and plan" (v. 5). We are chosen not because we are holy, but to become holy because of the Holy Spirit's work in our lives. Not because we are blameless, but to be made blameless through Christ.

Let this truth anchor your soul: you are not earning God's favor through your spiritual disciplines or specific actions. You are responding to Love that predates time itself. Your fasting, prayer, and acts of service spring from gratitude, not obligation.

In a season marked by self-examination and repentance, remember that you are already adopted as God's beloved daughter. This is where true transformation begins—not in striving, but in receiving the lavish grace of God poured out over you.

PRAYER

Gracious Father, in this season of Lent, remind me that I pray and seek You not to earn Your love, but to respond to it. Before time began, You chose me in love—not for what I've done, but for what You are doing in me through Christ. Help me rest in Your grace, walk in Your love, and be transformed by the Spirit's work. Thank You for calling me Yours. Amen.

How can you accept and live in the love God has for you?

How have you tried to earn God's love?

Before the creation of the world, God set His sights on You as the object of His love. How does this truth change how you see God? How you see yourself?

DAY 11
Let the Earth Keep Silent

Of what value is an idol, when its potter carves it,
    or a cast image that has been shaped?
It is a teacher of lies,
    for the potter trusts the pottery, though it is
    incapable of speaking.
Doom to the one saying to the tree, "Wake up!"
    or "Get up" to the silent stone.
Does it teach?
Look, it is overlaid with gold and silver,
    but there is no breath within it.
But the LORD is in his holy temple.
Let all the earth be silent before him.

Habakkuk 2:18-20

Sacred STILLNESS

In a world filled with noise and distraction, Habakkuk's words speak with stark clarity. In his time, he painted a vivid contrast between lifeless idols and the living God, a picture that illustrates our world today. Idols—those things that take a higher place than God in our lives—may appear to give us the life they want, but they are empty. Trusting them is trusting a lie, yet we chase after them in the form of success, approval, control, or even comfort.

The things around us promise security, but they cannot speak, guide, or save. They cannot answer our deepest questions or fill the hollow spaces in our souls. Only the Lord of the universe has true authority and life-giving power. His presence demands our attention and our reverent silence.

When we sit still before God, we recognize our limits and God's limitless glory. We stop chasing worthless gods, stop speaking, and begin listening. Lent invites us into this kind of silence—not empty, but full of awe. In stillness, we turn from lifeless idols and re-center our lives on the living God.

PRAYER

Almighty God of endless glory, draw me into Your holy silence and away from a world of noise and false promises. Give me the grace and desire to let go of idols that cannot speak or save—success, control, approval, power—and to rest in Your presence alone. Re-center my heart on You, the living God, who breathes life into the emptiness in my life. In stillness, help me listen, trust, and worship You with awe and surrender. Amen.

When you think of God in His holy temple (v. 20), what images, ideas, and emotions pop up for you?

What idols do you see people chase and seek out?

What idols have you believed in in the past, only to learn that God can meet your deepest needs?

DAY 12
Calm the Noise

You establish the mountains by your

strength;

you are dressed in raw power.

You calm the roaring seas;

  calm the roaring waves,

  calm the noise of the nations.

Psalm 65:6-7

We human beings can make it hard to hear God. Psalm 65 compares "the noise of the nations" (v. 7) with the turmoil of the roaring seas. The daily news bombards us with that deafening reality. Our noise makes it hard to remember who is in control and who has the power to address our unsettledness.

This psalm evokes God's presence and power in the abundant harvest, celebrated as the grain was gathered and the feasting began. After a long period of dryness and uncertainty, the people paused to remember the God who provided for their needs: prayers answered, sins forgiven, peace and security granted in times of fear.

How might we cut through the noise and recall all God does for us? What if we were to pause in the midst of our hectic lives and disconnect from our devices? In today's world, it can be a challenge to be still and recognize the wonder of the world around us—in a magnificent sunrise, the blessing of a spring rainstorm, or the unique creatures God crafted. Only by intentionally cultivating silence can we truly hear, listen to, and respond to God, but when we do we rediscover that God is in control of not only the seas but also our lives.

PRAYER

Lord, quiet the noise within and around me. In the chaos of the headlines and the daily demands of my life, help me pause and remember You are the One who provides, protects, forgives, and sustains. Give me the grace of noticing Your presence in beauty, nature, other people, silence, and stillness. Draw me into moments of wonder and gratitude. Let my heart rest in the truth that You are in control of the world—and my life too. Amen.

What noise interferes with your ability to hear God and respond to Him?

What chaotic waters are you navigating these days?

How has God shown up in this season of your life?

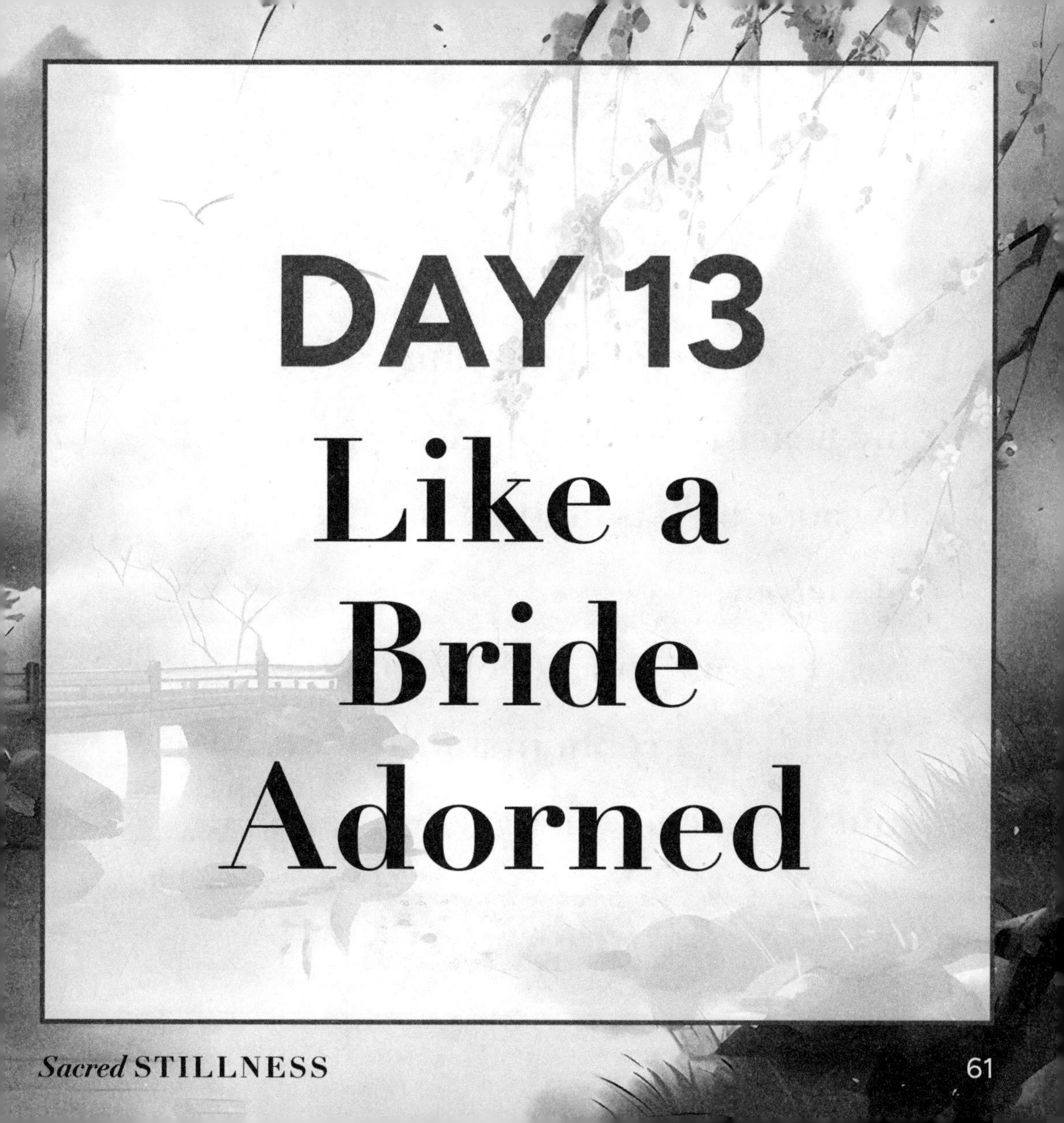

DAY 13

Like a Bride Adorned

I surely rejoice in the LORD;

my heart is joyful because of my God,

because he has clothed me with clothes

of victory,

wrapped me in a robe of righteousness

like a bridegroom in a priestly crown,

and like a bride adorned in jewelry.

Isaiah 61:10

At the beginning of His ministry, Jesus was asked to read from the Torah in the synagogue on the Sabbath. When given the scroll of Isaiah He found and read from Isaiah 61 (as we know it today) and told the crowd that He had fulfilled the prophecy (Luke 4:17-21). He brought good news to the poor and sight to the blind, let the oppressed go free, and proclaimed release to captives.

These songs of promise to Zion (Isaiah 60–62) depict a people who have been remarried to God (62:3-5), a bride beautifully adorned for Himself (Isa 61:10), a people who would become mediators of God's blessings to other nations. For the Israelites, these chapters incited faith in and faithfulness to God and offered hope for the future.

Passages like these can stir up a renewed trust in God and hope for our lives today. He calls us His bride. He frees us from the captivity of sin, breaks strongholds, clothes us in His righteousness, and creates beauty in the ashes of our lives. As we embrace His love, we can also proclaim freedom to captives, sight to the blind, and healing for the wounded. We can be recipients of His grace as well as proclaimers of it.

PRAYER

Lord, in a world that emphasizes status, power, wealth, and domination, it's easy for me to feel invisible, less-than, and insignificant. This passage reminds me that You call me Your bride and You clothe me with joy that stems from Your grace, love, and forgiveness. You have rescued me and set me free. As I encounter people in my daily life, give me the courage to proclaim the forgiveness and freedom You offer so others can experience Your redeeming power too. Amen.

How do you feel knowing that God calls you His precious bride?

Sacred STILLNESS

Who in your sphere of influence needs to hear that God wants to rescue and redeem them?

How might you share this good news in a winsome way?

DAY 14
Before All Things

Because all things were created by him:
    both in the heavens and on the earth,
    the things that are visible and the things
    that are invisible.
        Whether they are thrones or powers
        or rulers or authorities,
    all things were created through him and
    for him.

He existed before all things,
    and all things are held together in him.

Colossians 1:16-17

When life feels chaotic or uncertain, these verses offer profound reassurance. Christ is not only the agent of creation; He is the very one who sustains it. Everything visible and invisible—every structure, system, and soul—was created through Him and exists for Him. And what's more, all things are held together in Him. Not some things. Not only spiritual things. All things.

This means your life, with all its complexities, is not adrift. The same Christ who formed the stars holds your story. The same One who reigns over rulers also sees your unseen burdens. You are not forgotten or overlooked—you are sustained by the One who spoke the universe into being and who created you with intention and design. You have purpose and your life matters.

During seasons like Lent, we are invited to return to the center: to Christ Himself. As we strip away distractions and reflect on His sacrifice, we remember who He truly is—not just Savior, but Creator and Sustainer. He is the One who holds the universe—and our lives—in His hands.

PRAYER

Jesus, You are Creator and Sustainer of all things, including the details of my life. When my world feels chaotic and uncertain, remind me that You hold everything together. The same purposeful hands that formed the stars shape my present and my future. You know my hidden burdens and unspoken fears, and You want to help me through them. In this season of reflection, help me center my heart on You—my purpose, my hope, and my peace. Amen.

What hidden burdens and unspoken fears do you need to entrust to God?

What does it mean to you that Jesus holds all things together?

How have you seen Jesus hold you together during difficult times?

DAY 15
He Will Fight for You

But Moses said to the people, "Don't be afraid. Stand your ground, and watch the LORD rescue you today. The Egyptians you see today you will never ever see again. The LORD will fight for you. You just keep still."

Exodus 14:13-14

Picture the scene: the Israelites are trapped between the Red Sea and Pharaoh's advancing army. Panic fills their hearts as they face what seems like certain destruction. Yet in this moment of terror, Moses delivers one of Scripture's most powerful promises: "Don't be afraid. Stand your ground, and watch the LORD rescue you today."

When we're cornered by impossible situations—financial ruin, broken relationships, health crises, or crushing disappointments—our instinct is to frantically search for escape routes or fight with our own strength. But Moses commands something counterintuitive: "Be still." This isn't passive resignation but active faith—positioning ourselves to witness God's power unleashed on our behalf. Then Moses offers a promise: "The LORD will fight for you."

Sometimes our greatest act of faith isn't doing more but standing still long enough to see God work. Whatever impossible circumstance you're facing, remember: your rescue is coming. Stand firm, be still, and watch God fight for you.

PRAYER

God, when I feel anxious, remind me that I cannot overcome fear by my own power, but by trusting in You to provide for me and fight for me. Only through You can I be victorious. Exchange my weakness for Your strength and my doubt for faith in You. When I am tempted to take matters into my own hands, give me the grace to be still and wait for You to act. Amen.

What would it mean for God to fight for you?

Recall a time when God delivered you out of an impossible situation. Write about it below.

How can this experience give you hope and courage for situations you may be facing now?

DAY 16

When You Drift Away from God

Yet even now, says the LORD,
    return to me with all your hearts,
        with fasting, with weeping, and with
        sorrow;
tear your hearts
        and not your clothing.
    Return to the LORD your God,
        for he is merciful and compassionate,
        very patient, full of faithful love,
           and ready to forgive.

Joel 2:12-13

There are moments in every woman's life when we realize we've drifted away from God. We are caught up in busyness. Expectations of others (and ourselves) overwhelm us. We feel the weight of poor choices and misplaced priorities. The words of Joel offer us a tender yet urgent invitation: "Even now. . . return to me with all your hearts."

God isn't asking for a performance. He doesn't want us to offer empty gestures or outward displays. He wants our real, honest, weary, longing, hurting hearts. When Joel wrote, "tear your hearts and not your clothing," he was referring to the ancient practice of tearing one's clothing to show grief. Using this in a different context, Joel understood that someone could tear their garments without a changed heart. God sees beyond the outward action. He desires transformation.

During Lent, we often give up things to draw closer to God. But those outward actions mean little if they do not reflect a change in our hearts. Returning to God means giving Him our brokenness, our pride, and our need for control. This is the deeper fast He desires—letting go of the idols, beliefs, and wounds that keep us from Him.

God's invitation is full of hope. He wants to extend grace, compassion, abounding love. You only need to turn toward Him.

PRAYER

Lord, You call me to return to You, not with empty gestures but with my real, honest, sin-affected heart. I know You want to deal with the deeper issues inside—my hubris, unforgiveness, judgment, prejudice, emotional scars, and trauma. Take my brokenness and heal me gently. Help me release the idols and wounds that keep me from You. Transform me through Your Spirit. I turn toward Your grace, compassion, and abounding love. Amen.

What deeper issues of your heart might God want to address?

When you read that God "is merciful and compassionate, very patient, full of faithful love, and ready to forgive," what thoughts and emotions surface for you?

Are you hesitant to return to God with all your heart? Explain.

DAY 17
Balancing Devotion and Service

The Lord answered, "Martha, Martha, you are worried and distracted by many things. One thing is necessary. Mary has chosen the better part. It won't be taken away from her."

Luke 10:41-42

In the well-known story of Mary and Martha, Jesus visited the home of these two sisters. Mary sat at His feet, listening intently. Martha, meanwhile, was busy with the many tasks of hospitality that their culture demanded. When she asked Jesus to tell Mary to help her, He responded gently: "Martha, Martha, you are worried and distracted by many things. One thing is necessary."

It's easy to pit Mary and Martha against each other—as if one chose right and the other was wrong. But both women loved Jesus. Both welcomed Him. Martha wasn't rebuked for serving; she was gently invited to rest. Jesus saw her heart—anxious, pulled in many directions—and reminded her of what matters most: being with Him.

Many of us live Martha-shaped lives. We carry responsibilities, care for others, and often feel stretched thin. Jesus doesn't shame our service; He simply calls us to anchor it in His presence. Like Mary, we need stillness. Like Martha, we bring our gifts. Together, the sisters show us a full picture of devotion: worship through listening and loving through action.

Lent is a perfect season to embrace both. Sit at His feet. Serve from His strength. Let the many things give way to the things that truly matter.

PRAYER

Jesus, sometimes I am like Martha, and I get distracted by my tasks and service to others. And sometimes I am like Mary, and I long to sit at Your feet in stillness. I need Your Spirit to show me how to balance these two tendencies. Let me anchor my service in Your presence. Teach me to worship through listening and to love through action. In this season of Lent, let the many things give way to what truly matters: returning to You. Amen.

Which sister resonates with you the most, Mary or Martha? Why?

What would it look like for you to sit at Jesus's feet listening to Him?

How might you express your love for Jesus in serving others?

DAY 18
Let Your Heart Take Courage!

But I have sure faith

that I will experience the LORD's goodness

in the land of the living!

Hope in the LORD!

Be strong! Let your heart take courage!

Hope in the LORD!

Psalm 27:13-14

She has no name. The Gospel writer gives her labels like "Syrophoenician" (Mark 7:26) and "Canaanite" (Matt 15:22), and he compares her to a "dog" (Matthew 15:26). Her story is powerful. She went to Jesus because her daughter was sick. The lack of name would not get in the way of this woman's all-out desire to find someone who would (and could) heal her daughter. Insults meant nothing in the face of a mom on a mission.

This woman challenged labels and subverted cultural norms, and she is a model of bravery. She went toe-to-toe with Jesus (in front of everyone around them) in an unusual exchange that may not make sense to modern readers. Whether or not we fully understand their conversation, we know the power of labels. They leave us feeling less-than, inferior, and small. We shrink back, but not this woman. She charged ahead and Jesus honored her for it. She shows us what it means to let our hearts take courage in God.

PRAYER

Lord, I want to be like this woman who was fierce in her love and her faith. When doubt creeps in and circumstances overwhelm me, strengthen my weary soul. Let my heart take courage in Your faithfulness and your promises. Let me charge forward without fear because I know You are my refuge and strength. I will put my hope in You. Amen.

What would it be like for you to demonstrate the same bravery as the woman in this story?

In what areas of your life do you need to be courageous?

Who in your life is an example of courageous trust in God?

DAY 19
Act, Love, Walk

He has told you, human one, what is good and

what the LORD requires from you:

to do justice, embrace faithful love,

and walk humbly with your God.

Micah 6:8

What the Lord requires of us is simple yet far more complex than we like to admit. To "do justice" demands that we take action to promote peace and to right the wrongs when and where we can. To "embrace faithful love" is to demonstrate mercy because God has been merciful to us. And to "walk humbly" with God implies that we recognize that God is in control and we are not.

Coretta Scott King lived a life committed to these values. She walked alongside her husband (and humbly with God) through the civil rights movement. After Dr. King's death, she continued their work, establishing the Martin Luther King Jr. Center for Nonviolent Social Change. Throughout the remainder of her life, she worked for racial and economic justice, including civil rights for women, children, and every person regardless of sexual orientation. She advocated for environmental justice, employment, health, and education rights, and she was a lifelong advocate for world peace. Coretta Scott King's life is a testament to what God requires of us—to act on behalf of justice, to live out mercy, and to walk with God in humility.

PRAYER

Lord, I confess that I don't always know how to do justice, embrace faithful love, and walk humbly with You. I want to live in a way that honors You and the people around me. Show me the injustices around me and how to participate in undoing the wrongs. Let me be a person who is merciful to people, even when they don't share my politics or beliefs. I recognize that I can only do these things if I continually return to You in humility, so help me stay close to You. Amen.

Which of these commands—to do justice, act in mercy, or walk humbly with God— is the most challenging for you to live out?

Are there other women like Coretta Scott King who can serve as a role model for you? Describe the traits you want to learn from them.

In the space below, write your own prayer of commitment to live out the commands of Micah 6:8.

DAY 20
By His Power, Not Yours

His divine power has given us everything needed for life and godliness, through the knowledge of him who called us by his own glory and excellence. Thus he has given us, through these things, his precious and very great promises, so that through them you may escape from the corruption that is in the world because of lust and may become participants of the divine nature.

2 Peter 1:3-4, NRSVue

Lent is a time when we become acutely aware of our limitations—our struggles with temptation, our distractions in prayer, our longing for spiritual depth. But Peter reminds us that we don't walk this journey empty-handed.

"His divine power has given us everything needed." Not some things. Everything. Through Christ, we have access to the strength, wisdom, and grace required to live faithfully—even through the hard realities of life. This doesn't mean we always feel capable, composed, or strong. It means that the power of Christ is within reach through our relationship with Him.

Lent reminds us of Christ's sacrifice, but it can also remind us of the life He makes possible. Through the Holy Spirit's work, we are being continually transformed into women who reflect the character of Christ. But it's important to remember that it's His divine power at work in us, not our own.

Are you feeling stretched, weary, or inadequate these days? You're not alone—and you are not without help. God has already placed within you everything you need—because He's given you Himself.

PRAYER

Lord, in this season, remind me that though I feel stretched, weary, and inadequate, I am never alone. You have already given me everything I need through Your divine power. Strengthen my heart, quiet my anxiety, and draw me into deeper trust. Transform me by Your Spirit to reflect the beauty and character of Jesus. Amen.

Which of God's promises do you cling to when you feel depleted and unable to keep going?

What sinful cravings trip you up and keep you from living a life of godliness?

Reflect on your journey of faith in recent years. How have you been led to be more like God?

DAY 21

What Not to Do When You Pray

"But when you pray, go to your room, shut the door, and pray to your Father who is present in that secret place. Your Father who sees what you do in secret will reward you."

"When you pray, don't pour out a flood of empty words, as the Gentiles do. They think that by saying many words they'll be heard. Don't be like them, because your Father knows what you need before you ask."

Matthew 6:6-8

Lent invites us into practices like fasting, prayer, and self-examination. But in a world that often praises outward spirituality, Jesus's words in Matthew 6 remind us that the heart matters more than the show.

Praying isn't done for the approval of others; it's for deepening our intimacy with God. Jesus doesn't say if we pray, but when. He assumes we will practice this discipline, not as performance, but as private devotion. This isn't to say that we never engage in public prayer or offer a prayer in the presence of others. However, when we are in public, we need to focus on the content of our prayer and the God to whom we pray—instead of the people around us.

Whether you are praying in public or private, let it be an honest, authentic conversation between you and God. Don't worry about doing it "perfectly." Instead, let prayer draw you closer to the heart of the One who knows it all—the unseen hunger, the silent prayers, the private surrender. He sees it all and He meets you there.

PRAYER

Jesus, teach me to pray with a humble heart, not to impress others but to draw near to You. In both quiet corners and public spaces, let my words be honest, my motives pure, and my focus fixed on You alone. Thank You for seeing my hidden struggles and deepest needs and meeting them with Your grace, love, and provision. Amen.

As you reflect on both your public prayer and private prayer, how are they similar? How are they different?

Are you comfortable with praying in public? Explain.

What questions or struggles do you encounter when you pray in public or in private?

DAY 22
Honest Encounters with Jesus

"But the hour is coming, and is now here, when the true worshipers will worship the Father in spirit and truth, for the Father is seeking such people to worship him."

John 4:23 ESV

The Samaritan woman serves as an example of an honest encounter with Jesus. Rather than seek Jesus secretly, she spoke to Jesus at noon, out in the open and in the brightest light. Second, she engaged Jesus in a deep theological conversation. She wrestled with her understanding of God (notice how well she knew her tradition and her scriptures) and when prodded by Jesus, she talked about the real issues of her heart. Third, after encountering Jesus in a life-changing way, she left her jar, her chief source of water (and life), and immediately became the first evangelist in the Gospel of John. She invited others to "come and see" Jesus for themselves (John 4:29).

Unfortunately, the Samaritan is often misinterpreted. She is often labeled as a woman of loose morals, but notice that she had husbands, not customers. Furthermore, it's important to understand that she served in a representative role for the people of Samaria. As the ultimate bridegroom in her life (wells were associated with many betrothal scenes in the Old Testament), Jesus represented the potential for healing and wholeness for all believers who come to him. This unnamed woman showed how God can transform our lives when we come to Him honestly.

Sacred STILLNESS

PRAYER

Lord Jesus, thank You for meeting me where I am, just like You met the woman at the well. Help me to come to You honestly, ready to wrestle with truth and willing to engage with the deeper issues of my heart. Guide me to worship You in spirit and in truth. Help my life, like hers, bear witness to who You are as I encourage others to "come and see" the One who offers wholeness, freedom, and living water. Amen.

Do you find it easy to be honest and open with Jesus? Explain.

What is your water jar? In other words, what do you need to leave behind to follow Jesus?

How might you testify to the ways Jesus has worked in your life?

DAY 23

Better Than Life Itself

My lips praise you

    because your faithful love

    is better than life itself!

So I will bless you as long as I'm alive;

    I will lift up my hands in your name.

Psalm 63:3-4

David penned these words from the wilderness of Judea, likely when he was being hunted by King Saul. Stripped of the comforts of home, separated from the temple (where he met with God), facing an uncertain future, he declares an unshakable conviction: God's faithful love is better than life itself.

What a radical claim! Life is precious and beautiful, the sum of all our experiences and relationships. Yet David discovered something better—the resolute, unshakable love of God that transcends circumstances and outlasts trials. It is constant and steadfast when everything else falters.

During Lent, we enter our own kind of wilderness. We temporarily set aside certain comforts and pleasures, not because they are evil, but to rediscover what truly sustains us. In the emptiness, we often find what truly fills us.

David's response to recognizing God's surpassing love was active worship that was not dependent on favorable circumstances. It was worship anchored in God's unchanging, unfailing love. May we also discover that God's love is our deepest need and greatest treasure.

PRAYER

Jesus, your love is better than anything this world could offer me. I admit, though, that sometimes I chase after false love and look for other things to sustain my soul. Forgive my wayward heart. Satisfy the deepest longings in my heart, and let me trust that your love never fails. Amen.

What do you turn to as a substitute for God's love?

How can God's love be better than life?

How has God satisfied the deepest longings in your heart?

DAY 24
Faith
as a Gift

You are saved by God's grace because of your faith. This salvation is God's gift. It's not something you possessed. It's not something you did that you can be proud of. Instead, we are God's accomplishment, created in Christ Jesus to do good things. God planned for these good things to be the way that we live our lives.

Ephesians 2:8-10

Grace is God's unmerited love, favor, mercy, and action in our lives. It's by this grace that we receive new life in Christ. God's grace pardons us for the things we did wrong and empowers us to grow day by day in the image of Christ. By grace we are forgiven, healed, redeemed, restored, transformed, and made alive. By grace we are saved!

Grace is countercultural in a merit-based, achievement-driven society. We strive to prove our worth as good wives, mothers, sisters, daughters, employees, friends, neighbors, and church members. If we are not careful, these same cultural tendencies can influence how we understand our relationship with God. We may despair that we are not "good enough" to be saved. We may fall into thinking we need to prove our worthiness or earn God's favor. Ephesians 2 reminds us that God's merciful action in our lives does not occur because we deserve it or earn it.

We are saved by grace because God deeply loves us. As recipients of this lavish gift, may we in turn be bold in extending grace to those around us.

PRAYER

Merciful God, thank You for the gift of grace You offer—unearned, undeserved, and freely given. In a world that tells me to prove my worth and value, remind me that Your love isn't earned but received. I cannot do anything to make You love me less, and I cannot do anything to make You love me more—because Your love is perfect and steadfast. By Your grace, I am forgiven, healed, and made alive in Christ. May I draw others to You because of Your love in my life. Amen.

What does it mean for you to know that God's love for you is steadfast and perfect?

Reread these verses. Let them sink in. Can you accept the grace of God as a gift? Why or why not?

What might be some good things God planned for you and created you to do?

DAY 25
All Are Welcome

He made a whip from ropes and chased them all out of the temple, including the cattle and the sheep. He scattered the coins and overturned the tables of those who exchanged currency. He said to the dove sellers, "Get these things out of here! Don't make my Father's house a place of business."

John 2:15-16

People contrast the "loving" God of the New Testament with the "angry" God of the Old Testament. We are very uncomfortable with the idea of a wrathful God, ready to wipe out human beings for their sins. What about forgiveness? What about grace?

We forget that Jesus got angry at the injustice and idolatry he saw right before his eyes, especially when practiced by religious leaders. Remember how he turned over the tables of the money changers in the temple courts (John 2:13-16)? These courts were the place where non-Jews could worship, but they had become a marketplace instead. The temple itself was supposed to be a place where Jews could worship, offer sacrifices in keeping with the Law, and experience forgiveness. Instead, the money changers exploited the people with unfair exchange rates. Merchants took advantage of people who had traveled far distances and needed an animal for sacrifice, increasing the prices and making a huge profit. And none of the religious elite—Pharisees, Sadducees, teachers of the Law—spoke out against these practices.

Jesus's actions remind us that God desires justice, mercy, and honest worship. There is no place for religious show, favoritism, exploitation, or manipulation. The church is supposed to be a place where all are welcome and have a seat at the table of grace.

PRAYER

Lord, cleanse my heart as You cleansed the temple. Forgive me for any part I play in injustice or empty religion. Make my worship pure, my actions fair and just, and my home and church community welcoming. Help me reflect Your heart, full of mercy, justice, and grace, and help my church be a place where all are invited to the table to partake in Your grace. Amen.

How do Jesus's actions in the temple challenge your understanding of God's love?

Have you ever experienced or witnessed a church environment that felt more like a marketplace than a place of worship? Describe it.

How can you ensure your church remains a place of grace, welcome, and authentic worship?

DAY 26
The God Who Sings over You

The LORD your God is in your midst—
a warrior bringing victory.
He will create calm with his love;
he will rejoice over you with singing.

Zephaniah 3:17

Women were the central witnesses to the death and resurrection of Jesus. On the other hand, the disciples were absent and showed up after Easter only on the mountain as the women had instructed them. The women were present every step of the way. A woman anointed Jesus for burial (Matthew 26:6-12), Pilate's wife advocated for Jesus's life (27:19), the women held vigil with Jesus as he endured the cross (27:55), and they kept watch at the tomb (27:61). On the first Easter, Mary Magdalene and Mary returned to Jesus's grave to find the tomb empty and became the first evangelists of the gospel. He elevated the status of women in His dealings with them, which undoubtedly drew them to Him.

We can imagine the love and appreciation Jesus held for these women who followed Him so faithfully. No doubt He would rejoice over them with singing. We can also imagine ourselves bringing Jesus joy. His favor and love extend to us, calling us His beloved children. Can you hear the voice of Jesus singing over you, celebrating you and thanking His Father for you? He does!

Sacred STILLNESS

PRAYER

Jesus, thank You for seeing, honoring, and entrusting women with Your message. Just as You held these women in high esteem, help me believe that You value and prize me too. Give me the audacious faith to believe You rejoice over me too. Let me live from that love—courageous, faithful, and attentive to Your voice. May I bring You joy with my presence and devotion. Amen.

What is your response to reading that God rejoices over you with singing?

Have you ever felt unseen or unappreciated in your faith journey? How does Jesus's treatment of the women around Him speak to you?

How can you respond to Jesus's love with the same faithfulness the women showed?

DAY 27
Dying to Live

I have been crucified with Christ and I no longer live, but Christ lives in me. And the life that I now live in my body, I live by faith, indeed, by the faithfulness of God's Son, who loved me and gave himself for me.

Galatians 2:20

In Galatians 2:20, Paul described faithfulness as a dying to self in order to make God the center of our lives. We are crucified along with Christ, and in this crucifixion, we die and are replaced by Christ, who lives within us. Making Christ the center of our lives does require self-sacrifice, but this looks different from woman to woman.

For those of us with an abundance of resources and power, faithfulness may look like humbling ourselves and setting aside our preferences and pride to serve others.

For those of us who are regularly expected to give up our desires to those in power, faithfulness takes on a different pattern. Many women are not treated with the dignity that comes with being made in God's image. For them, following Christ looks more like setting aside self-hatred and fear and embracing the knowledge that they are beloved, like the disciples who allowed Christ to wash their feet.

For all of us, dying to ourselves and making God the center and focus of our lives means letting Christ's love reshape how we see ourselves and others.

PRAYER

Lord Jesus, thank You for dying for me and breathing new life into me. Teach me what dying to myself looks like in my life. Help me surrender daily so that You can live through my thoughts, words, and actions. Let my encounters with others reflect Your presence within me and may my life glorify You alone. I am Yours. Amen.

What does it look like for Christ to live in you?

What does "dying to self" mean for you in this season of life?

Where is God inviting you into deeper obedience right now?

DAY 28
Your Heart's Posture

"This people honors me with their lips, but their hearts are far away from me. Their worship of me is empty since they teach instructions that are human rules."

Matthew 15:8-9

In the biblical understanding, the heart is the seat of desires, intentions, expectations, and plans that determine a person's character and the direction of their behavior. The heart is the primary place where we encounter God and where God works to cause change, insight, and the transformation in our lives. Jesus understood this, which is why He described the religious leaders in such stark terms. While the Pharisees, Sadducees, and other religious leaders were supposed to help the people in their relationship with God, they made it worse. They created rule after rule to ensure God's Law was followed, and in doing so, they forgot to love God and care for people. Their example shows us what not to do to serve God faithfully.

Unfortunately, it is easy to make the same mistake that the religious leaders did. We can become so focused on doing all the right things—reading our Bibles every day, keeping prayer lists, going to church, serving others—that we can lose out on a deep connection with God. Our activities can dampen our love for God. Jesus reminded His followers (and us) to stay focused on what is most important—a heart connected to and shaped by God.

Sacred STILLNESS

PRAYER

Lord, guard my heart from becoming busy with religious activities but distant from You. Help me not get so caught up in doing the right things that I don't love You deeply and genuinely. Shape my desires, intentions, and choices so they reflect Your heart. Let me live with love and true devotion that is lived out in my actions. Amen.

How can good spiritual practices become obstacles to a genuine relationship with God?

What practices help you keep your heart soft and open to God?

In what ways do you sense God shaping your heart right now?

DAY 29
Finding God in the Silence

Oh, I must find rest in God only,

because my hope comes from him!

Only God is my rock and my salvation—

my stronghold!—I will not be shaken.

My deliverance and glory depend on God.

God is my strong rock.

My refuge is in God.

Psalm 62:5-7

Sacred STILLNESS

Life often feels relentless for women—pressures mount, demands from family chip away at our energy, and peace feels out of reach. In these verses, the psalmist gently redirects us with one simple yet powerful truth: rest is found in God alone. Not in success, security, relationships, or routines. Only in the steady presence of our Rock and Redeemer can we be at rest.

We are invited to this sacred stillness. When life shakes us, we can be confident that we are held. When hope feels fragile, God restores it. When we feel exposed or weak, God becomes our stronghold.

Resting in God doesn't mean inactivity; it means anchoring our souls in His faithfulness. It's an intentional choice to release control and take hold of His strength.

Take a breath. Let your soul settle. Place your hope again in the One who is unshakable.

PRAYER

Lord, my soul finds rest in You alone. When my life is overwhelming and I feel like I'm drowning, anchor me in Your presence. Be my rock, my refuge, and my salvation. Teach me to hope in You when everything else feels uncertain. Thank You for holding me secure, cared for, and loved. I choose to trust and rest in You today. Amen.

What areas of your life feel especially "shaken" right now?

Where do you sometimes look for rest or security besides God?

What does it mean for you to call God your "rock" and your "refuge"?

DAY 30
The Correct Fast

Is this the kind of fast I choose,
  a day of self-affliction,
  of bending one's head like a reed
  and of lying down in mourning
  clothing and ashes?
  Is this what you call a fast,
    a day acceptable to the LORD?

Isn't this the fast I choose:
  releasing wicked restraints, untying
  the ropes of a yoke,
  setting free the mistreated,
  and breaking every yoke?

Isaiah 58:5-6

During Lent, we often focus on personal sacrifice—giving up comforts, sweets, or poor habits—to help us draw nearer to God. But Isaiah 58 challenges us to broaden our understanding of true fasting. It isn't merely abstaining; it means taking action. It's about advocating for justice, standing up for the oppressed, and caring for those in need. Two women in the Old Testament—Puah and Shiphrah—serve as an example for us.

These two women served as midwives for the Hebrew community. Their story takes place when the Israelites had been living in Egypt for more than four hundred years (see Exodus 1). Pharaoh feared the Israelites because he thought they would threaten his power. He gave Puah and Shiphrah an impossible order: kill every newborn Hebrew baby boy (Exodus 1:16). Imagine their fear: the supreme leader of the country had given them a direct order. But the two midwives respected God and made the choice to ignore Pharaoh's order. God blessed their families (Exodus 1:20-21) because they chose the path of justice and the innate value of human life.

Lent challenges us to not only give something up but to also act on behalf of others. We can lighten someone's burden. We can feed someone facing food scarcity. We can step in for someone who is being mistreated. The point is, true fasting not only cleanses our hearts but it also opens them—to make space for loving God and others.

Sacred STILLNESS

PRAYER

God of justice and mercy, teach me to fast in a way that honors You—not just by letting go of sinful behaviors but also by working on the behalf of others. Give me the courage of Puah and Shiphrah to choose what is right, even when it's hard. Open my heart to both You and my neighbor, and help me act with compassion, boldness, and love. Amen.

In what ways might God be calling you to act on behalf of others this season?

What fears might be keeping you from standing up for others like Puah and Shiphrah did?

How can you use your voice, resources, and time to lighten someone's burden this week?

Sacred STILLNESS

DAY 31

Faith's Pioneer and Perfector

So then, with endurance, let's also run the race that is laid out in front of us, since we have such a great cloud of witnesses surrounding us. Let's throw off any extra baggage, get rid of the sin that trips us up, and fix our eyes on Jesus, faith's pioneer and perfecter. He endured the cross, ignoring the shame, for the sake of the joy that was laid out in front of him, and sat down at the right side of God's throne.

Hebrews 12:1-2

The Christian life is not a sprint—it's a marathon. Hebrews 12:1-2 paints a powerful image of endurance, purpose, and focus. We are not running aimlessly; we're following a path laid out by a loving God. And we're not alone. The "great cloud of witnesses"—believers who have gone before us—cheers us on with their lives of faith. Their testimonies remind us that God is faithful through every season.

To run well, though, we must lay things down. The passage urges us to release any "extra baggage" and the sin that entangles us. The weight of bitterness, comparison, fear, favoritism, past hurts, and sinful habits can zap us of our strength, slow us down, and even put us on the sideline temporarily.

The remedy is to fix our eyes on Jesus—the one who started our faith and will finish it. He endured the cross despite the shame and humiliation. His story shapes and directs ours. When we feel weary, we can look to Him as our ultimate example of endurance, hope, and victory. We can run this race with courage and determination, knowing the course laid out leads us to Him.

PRAYER

Jesus, you are the author and perfecter of my faith. Help me run with endurance, letting go of anything that slows me down. Strengthen me when I grow tired and fix my eyes on you when the path feels unclear. May your joy be my strength and your cross my compass. Thank you for walking before me and cheering me on through your Spirit. Amen.

What "extra baggage" might be weighing you down in your spiritual journey right now?

How can you intentionally fix your eyes on Jesus this week?

Who are the "cloud of witnesses" in your life—past or present—who cheer you on in your faith?

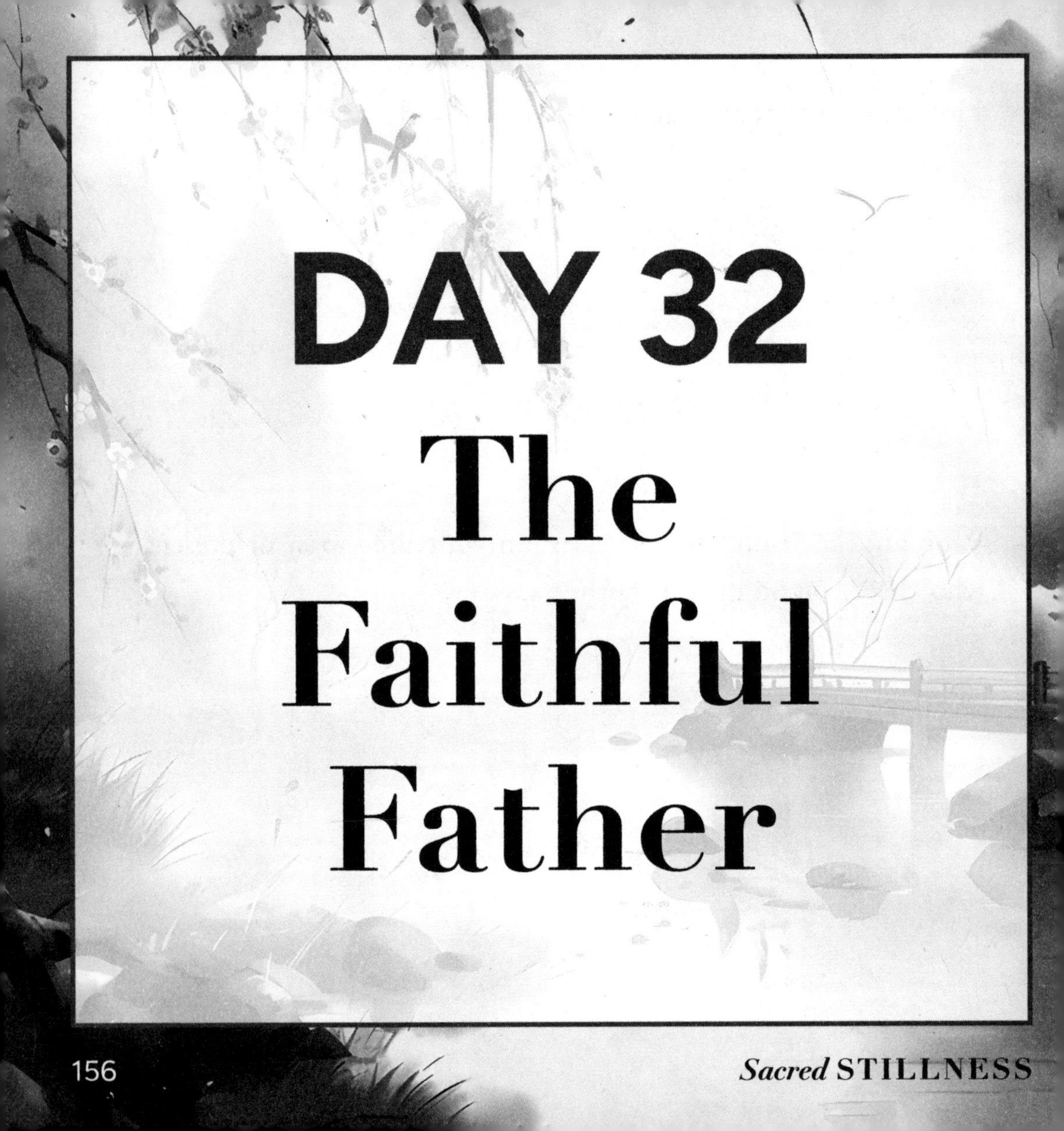

DAY 32

The Faithful Father

"While he was still a long way off, his father saw him and was moved with compassion. His father ran to him, hugged him, and kissed him."

Luke 15:20

Jesus often used parables to explain the heart of God. In Luke 15, He illustrated God's character through a story about a lost coin and a lost sheep (Luke 15:1-32), and a faithful father who loved a prodigal son. Unlike a lost coin or lost sheep, the lost son made deliberate choices that broke his father's heart, leaving his home to pursue extravagant living. When at the end of his rope (and his money) and he returns home to his father, there is no judgment upon his return. Instead, the faithful father put a ring on his finger, sandals on his feet, and a robe on his back.

There was no chastisement, no recounting of wrongs done, or shaming the son. There was embracing, welcoming, rejoicing—and a huge party, "because this son of mine was dead and has come back to life! He was lost and is found!" (15:24).

Our heavenly Father searches for us when we get lost, whether through ignorance, the harmful actions of others, or our own selfish choices; God's love is stronger than any wrong turn or painful consequence we experience. His grace lifts us up and calls us home, restoring us and celebrating our return. Then, perhaps sharing God's mercy, we will open our arms and hearts and minds to others who are far away from their heavenly Father.

PRAYER

Faithful Father, thank You for seeking me when I stray, loving me beyond my mistakes, and running toward me with grace when I turn back to You. Heal me with Your mercy and strengthen my trust in Your restoring love. Soften my heart to extend that same grace to others who feel far from You. May my life reflect Your open heart, grace, mercy, and forgiveness. Amen.

How have you experienced the Father's restorative grace when you strayed from Him?

What might be keeping you from fully receiving God's embrace and restoration today?

How can you be a living reflection of the Father's mercy and forgiveness to someone in your life?

DAY 33
How to Have Perfect Peace

Those with sound thoughts you will
keep in peace,
   in peace because they trust in you.
Trust in the LORD forever,
   for the LORD is a rock for all ages.

Isaiah 26:3-4

Sacred STILLNESS

Although this passage in Isaiah was written centuries before her birth, Mary, the mother of Jesus, lived out the truths in the prophet's words. When we first meet her in the Gospel of Luke, we find a young woman confused and afraid (Luke 1:29-30), facing an unexpected pregnancy with the burden of her society's shame for bearing a child outside of marriage (Matthew 1:18-25). Yet she consented to the work and will of God because she trusted in Him.

Perhaps we best get a sense of who Mary was and the faith she embodied by reading her own words (Luke 1:46-55). She gave thanks and glorified God for promising hope, mercy, and justice for her people—the poor, the powerless, the oppressed, and the disregarded. She was a young woman whose life was marked by trust in the One who could end the political violence and alleviate injustice in her world (and ours).

Mary's story reminds us that a life of faith will not shield us from danger, anxiety, loss, or grief. Yet her trust in God's faithfulness is a powerful model of surrender. Mary lived out a faith that was far from meek and mild. She lived out defiant trust that would carry her through the challenges that lay before her.

PRAYER

God of mercy and justice, thank You for Mary's courageous example of trust. When fear and uncertainty press in, help me respond with the same bold surrender. Show me how to glorify You even in hardship, to believe Your promises, and to remain steadfast in the unknown. Let my life reflect a defiant faith rooted in Your faithfulness and love. Like Mary, may I trust You with my whole heart. Amen.

How can Mary's trust in God challenge or strengthen your own faith today?

When have you felt fear or uncertainty like Mary did? What happened?

What helps you say yes to God, even when the path ahead is unclear?

DAY 34
Where to Look for Help

I raise my eyes toward the mountains.

Where will my help come from?

My help comes from the LORD,

the maker of heaven and earth.

Psalm 121:1-2

Where does your help come from?

Psalm 121 opens with this question, and it is worth pondering. The psalmist looked upward to the hills to find the answer, not because they were the source of help, but because they represented a powerful God: "My help comes from the Lord, the maker of heaven and earth."

The psalmist proclaimed that the One who had put the universe in motion watches over all His creation, and that same God cares for us today. He doesn't doze off or take breaks. He keeps his children from slipping; He is our shade, keeper, and protector.

These verses invite us to shift our gaze upward when we need help. In seasons of weariness, uncertainty, and fear, we can look inward or around us for relief, but our unfailing Creator and Sustainer sits enthroned in heaven. The One who made the mountains is the same One who walks beside us through every valley.

Today, let this psalm quiet your anxiety and steady your heart. God is not only able; He is willing and faithful to help when you turn to Him.

Sacred STILLNESS

PRAYER

God of creation, You are my helper and keeper and I lift my eyes to You. In every moment of fear or fatigue, remind me that You do not slumber or sleep or turn away. Thank You for being my constant protector, day and night, in my going out and coming in. Help me trust Your watchful care and rest in Your faithful presence. I place my life in Your hands. Amen.

How does knowing God watches over you personally change the way you face challenges?

Where do you typically look for help when you're in trouble or overwhelmed?

In what areas of your life do you need to release control and trust God's protection more fully?

DAY 35
Just as He Loved

"I give you a new commandment: Love each other. Just as I have loved you, so you also must love each other. This is how everyone will know that you are my disciples, when you love each other."

John 13:34-35

This chapter begins and ends with love. Jesus loved the disciples fully even though He knew everything about them, including the fact that one would betray and one would deny Him. This didn't stop Him from demonstrating that love. Like Mary, who anointed Jesus's feet, He attended to the care of their bodies in intimate, literally touching ways.

Having shown them what love looks like in practical and tangible ways, Jesus announced the standard for identifying a Christian. He didn't point to purity, Bible knowledge, or holiness; people will know believers by their love (John 15:9-17). He didn't mention moral perfection, scriptural knowledge, or religious status. The true mark of a disciple is self-sacrificing love.

This kind of love is radical. It goes beyond kindness and is lived out in action. It embraces those who disappoint us. It forgives those who wound us. It takes up the towel and kneels to serve, just like Jesus did.

If love is what identifies a follower of Christ, then how we treat others—especially when they betray or hurt us—matters deeply. Our love becomes our witness to the world that Jesus's love can change the world.

PRAYER

Jesus, teach me to love like You do—without condition and without pride. Help me to serve with humility, offer mercy, and to demonstrate compassion to others. Let love be more than my words; let it be the way I live. May others see You in how I treat them, especially when they hurt or mistreat me. Make my life a reflection of Your love. Amen.

Who has demonstrated Jesus's love to you in a personal, tangible way?

When you think about being "known by your love," what areas in your life reflect this well?

Who in your life is hard to love right now—and how might Jesus be calling you to love them?

DAY 36
How's Your Attitude?

Don't do anything for selfish purposes, but with humility think of others as better than yourselves. Instead of each person watching out for their own good, watch out for what is better for others. Adopt the attitude that was in Christ Jesus.

Philippians 2:3-5

Lent calls us to journey with Jesus toward the cross, following His path of self-sacrificial love. Paul's description of Jesus in these verses shows us how to imitate Him—in the countercultural choice of other-centered service.

The phrase "selfish purposes" reminds us that even in serving, we can focus on ourselves. We can fast with a prideful heart, serve with an attitude of superiority, or give to make us look good. But Paul points us to Jesus's mindset, one that focuses on others.

To "think of others as better than yourselves" does not mean self-hatred or abandoning self-care. It's the revolutionary act of seeing others through God's eyes, recognizing their inherent worth and dignity. That perspective can then motivate us into tangible action in the behalf of others.

During this season, ask God to show you whether your spiritual practices are drawing you into humility and love for others. Spiritual growth isn't about insulating ourselves from the world; it's learning to kneel lower, serve more freely, and love sacrificially.

PRAYER

Lord Jesus, as I journey toward the cross in this season, transform my heart to mirror Your self-sacrificial love. Strip away my prideful motivation and forgive my selfish attitudes. Help me see others the way You do, recognizing their worth and dignity as Your beloved children. Let my spiritual practices draw me deeper into humility and genuine care for others as I let Your sacrifice move me to serve others authentically. Amen.

What specific ways can you follow Jesus's example of self-sacrificial love in your daily relationships, even if it's costly or uncomfortable?

What does it mean for you to adopt an attitude like Christ? What might that look like?

Are you willing to make sacrifices in your day-to-day life to fulfill God's dreams and purposes for you? Explain.

DAY 37

Finding a Hope That Does Not Disappoint

But not only that! We even take pride in our problems, because we know that trouble produces endurance, endurance produces character, and character produces hope. This hope doesn't put us to shame, because the love of God has been poured out in our hearts through the Holy Spirit, who has been given to us.

Romans 5:3-5

In everyday conversation, hope indicates a feeling that things are likely to turn out well, like "I hope this meeting will be short" or "I hope I don't run out of gas." In Christian theology, hope is not tied to an outcome. It's tied to God's character. It is choosing to live in the light of God's eternal love and faithfulness. As a virtue, it is both a blessing from God and a daily (or moment-by-moment) choice. It's both a noun and a verb, a gift and a practice. Faith in God is the root of hope, and hope is lived out in love.

Biblical hope affirms that the world is held in the hands of a God who is greater than any trouble and can conquer even death. This means the future can be different from the past, and the present—however grim—still leads to a future directed by God's power and love.

Real hope is centered on God alone. Setting our hope on anything or anyone will ultimately disappoint.

PRAYER

Faithful God, anchor my hope in You and Your unchanging character and not in any faulty foundation. When circumstances seem grim, help me choose to live in the confidence of Your eternal love and faithfulness. Root my hope deeply in You alone, knowing You alone hold the world in Your hands and can conquer even death. Amen.

How has God shown Himself as your secure hope?

How can you distinguish between worldly hope (wanting favorable outcomes) and biblical hope (trusting in God's character)?

How can you cultivate deeper hope in God?

DAY 38

Do You Believe Him?

Jesus said to her, "I am the resurrection and the life. Whoever believes in me will live, even though they die. Everyone who lives and believes in me will never die. Do you believe this?"

She replied, "Yes, Lord, I believe that you are the Christ, God's Son, the one who is coming into the world."

John 11:25-27

In this famous story of Lazarus's death, Martha and Mary sent word to Jesus, asking for help for their beloved brother. Remarkably, He did not rush to the scene; He intentionally tarried. How does this mesh with the express statement that "Jesus loved Martha, her sister, and Lazarus" (John 11:5)? Both sisters confronted Jesus for not coming sooner and preventing Lazarus's death. Both of them spoke honestly, "Lord, if you had been here, my brother wouldn't have died" (John 11:21, 32).

We can be like these grieving women. How much time do we spend on the "if" game, wondering about what could have been if God had intervened when we asked? What if He had . . . ? If God cared, He would have . . . ? Why didn't God . . . ?

Rather than focus on the reasons for His delay, Jesus pointed Martha to a greater reality: He is life and that life is always available. In the end, Martha understood (at least as much as she could), so much so that she said, "Yes, Lord, I believe that you are the Christ, God's Son, the one who is coming into the world" (John 11:27; echoed in John 20:31).

That's just who Jesus is—the One coming into our world and seeking us out. Every moment of every day is ripe with the promise of resurrection and life.

PRAYER

Jesus, You are the Resurrection and the Life. When I question Your timing or wonder why You don't respond like I want, help me trust that Your love remains steady and true. Give me the faith to hold on to the greater truth of who You are when my world turns upside down. In my grief or confusion, anchor me in hope and faith that You are always drawing me near, offering me resurrection and life. Amen.

In what areas of your life do you need to trust that Jesus offers resurrection and life, not what you think is best?

How do you usually respond to disappointment or unanswered prayer?

In the space below, write a prayer to God about something you need Him to do. Be as honest with Him as Mary and Martha.

DAY 39

Be Encouraged, Daughter

Then a woman who had been bleeding for twelve years came up behind Jesus and touched the hem of his clothes. She thought, If I only touch his robe I'll be healed. When Jesus turned and saw her, he said, "Be encouraged, daughter. Your faith has healed you." And the woman was healed from that time on.

Matthew 9:20-22

After Jesus was summoned to the home of a ruler whose daughter had just died, we meet an unnamed woman who had been bleeding for twelve long years.

Though the ruler showed faith in coming to Jesus, Matthew pointed out this woman's remarkable, risky faith. She did not even try to talk to Jesus; she believed that merely touching His hem could heal her. She was reluctant to come to him face-to-face, but Jesus turned toward her in response to her touch.

This season offers cleaning and healing of a different kind. When we turn our hearts toward Jesus, we can claim the forgiveness He offers and give Him our wounded hearts. Like the woman in this story, we can experience His powerful healing and the new life He brings. Be encouraged, beloved daughter of God. He sees you reaching out to Him and He will not turn you away.

PRAYER

Jesus, You see me even when I feel invisible, ashamed, or unworthy. Thank You for responding to the cries of my desperate heart. Just like the woman who reached for Your hem, I am reaching out to You in faith, bringing You my brokenness and hurts. Turn toward me, Lord, and make me whole. You are my Healer and my Savior. Amen.

How does the woman's silent but daring faith challenge or inspire my own?

What parts of your life or story feel too broken to bring to Jesus?

What would it look like for you to reach out to Jesus like the woman in this story?

DAY 40
The God Who Doesn't Forget

Listen to me, O house of Jacob,

　all the remnant of the house of Israel,

who have been borne by me from your birth,

　carried from the womb;

even to your old age I am he;

　even when you turn gray I will carry you.

I have made, and I will bear;

　I will carry and will save.

Isaiah 46:3-4 NRSVue

Tucked away in the Bible is the little-known story of Bilhah, the maidservant of Rachel, Jacob's wife. Rachel was desperate for children and could not conceive, so she forced her maidservant Bilhah to become a surrogate mother. Rachel gave Bilhah to her husband and then took the children as her own.

How hollow Bilhah must have felt. As those boys grew, we can wonder whether Rachel's parenting style irritated Bilhah or if she was forced to nanny the children that once grew in her womb. Did her heart ache to be the first to respond when one of them skinned his knees? Did she long for those children to call her Mom?

While Rachel claimed two of the children that Bilhah bore, God knew what had happened. He had not forgotten Bilhah. In Genesis 35:25, where the Bible lists Jacob's descendants, Bilhah's sons are credited under her name, not Rachel's. God's final word gave justice to a woman otherwise forgotten in her culture.

This passage in Isaiah speaks of another parent. Our heavenly Father cared for us in the womb and continues to carry us even into our old age. He has made us, and He will bear us; He will carry and will save us, no matter what others do.

PRAYER

God of justice and compassion, thank You for seeing the overlooked and honoring the forgotten. You knew Bilhah's story, her sorrow, and her silent anguish. When others ignore or mistreat me, You remain my faithful Sustainer and Defender. Carry the hidden hurts I bear. Help me rest in Your lasting love, trusting that You will not forsake or forget me. Amen.

What silent burdens are you carrying that you need to entrust to God?

Have you ever felt unseen, overlooked, or taken for granted like Bilhah might have?

How does knowing that God credited Bilhah with her children bring you comfort or hope?

Abingdon *Women*™

WE ARE HERE TO SERVE YOUR LIFE AND FAITH!

Our studies and books are designed for Christian women of all ages and stages of life who are looking for inspiration and encouragement as they navigate the ups and downs of life. From personal faith topics to devotionals and more, our studies and books help women live in the Word as they live in the world.

Explore more at AbingdonWomen.com!